DEDICATED TO MY BEAUTIFUL
NIECE MISS ELLA-ROSE
EVERYDAY IS RAINBOWS AND
UNICORNS WHEN IM WITH YOU

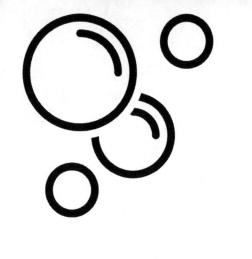

"LITTLE EXPLORER, HIDDEN WITHIN THESE PAGES ARE MAGICAL SECRETS JUST FOR YOU. CAN YOU FIND THEM ALL?"

THIS BOOK BELONGS TO:

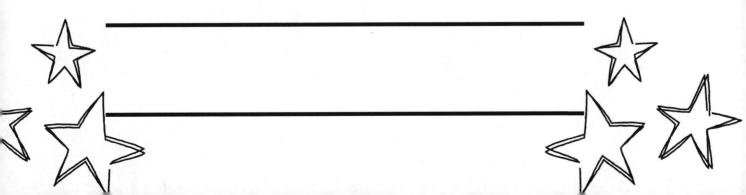

"SHINE BRIGHT,
LITTLE STAR"

COLOUR PALETTE

"YOU ARE BRAVE"

"YOU ARE LOVED"

"YOU ARE BRIGHT"

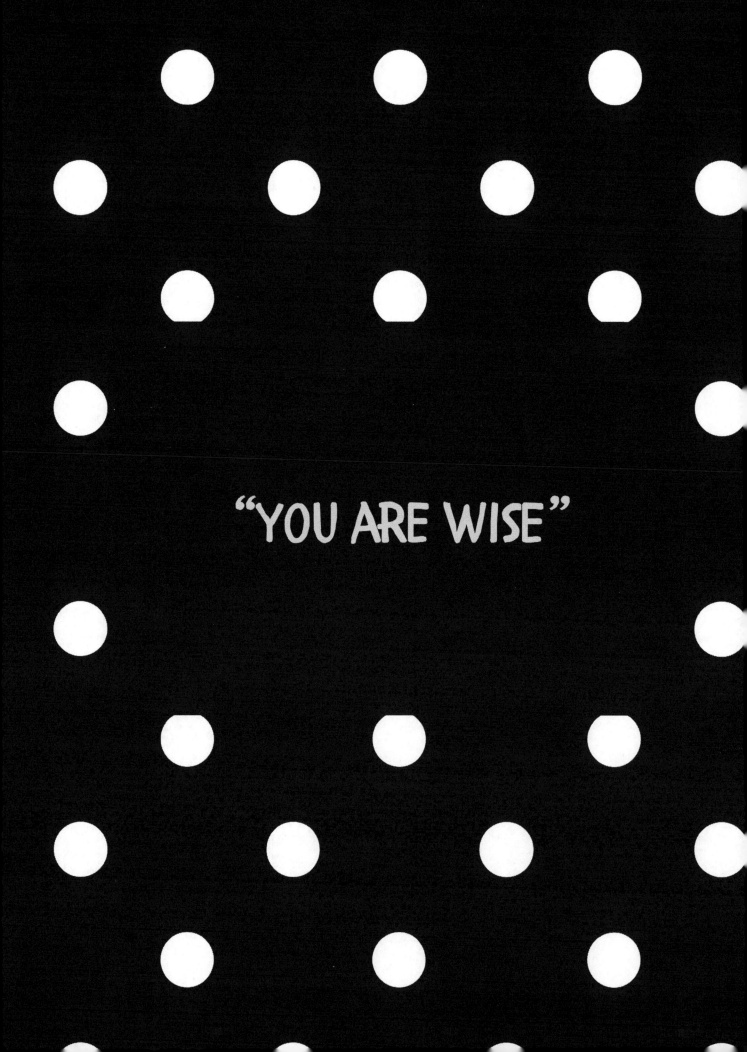

"YOU ARE WISE"

"YOU CAN BE ANYTHING
YOU DREAM OF"

"YOU CAN BE
ANYTHING"

"DANCE, SING & LOVE
AS LOUD AS YOU CAN"

"YOU ARE BRAVE"

"BE YOUR OWN KIND
OF BEAUTIFUL"

"SHINE BRIGHT WITH
ALL YOUR MIGHT"

"FLY HIGH,
LITTLE BUTTERFLY"

"DREAM, SPARKLE, REPEAT"

"FILLED WITH COURAGE,
WRAPPED IN KINDNESS"

"YOUR SMILE LIGHTS
UP THE WORLD"

"DREAMS ARE WHISPERS
FROM YOUR HEART"

"FOREVER RAINBOWS
AND FAIRY DUST"

"YOU ARE A KIND FRIEND"

"SMILE UNTIL YOUR
CHEEKS HURT"

"YOU ARE LOVED
MORE THAN YOU WILL
EVER KNOW"

"DANCE LIKE A
MAGICAL FAIRY"

"YOU CAN DO ANYTHING"

THANK YOU FOR BRINGING THE MAGICAL UNICORNS BACK TO COLOR

PLEASE SHARE YOUR WORKS OF ART TO OUR FACEBOOK GROUP - LILY BEE PUBLISHING

THERE WILL BE SPOT PRIZES FOR THE MOST CREATIVE WORK AND FREE DOWNLOADS

WE WOULD LOVE TO KNOW
YOUR THOUGHTS.
A GREAT WAY TO SEND FEEDBACK AND
PICTURES OF YOUR COLORING IS TO
CLICK THIS LINK HERE!

WE WILL BE BACK WITH
ANOTHER MAGICAL COLORING
BOOK SOON!!